```
            LIFE

  DE              DE
  SIRE    I       SIRE

          WILL
          S
          E
INNER     E         OUTER
          K
          
  DE              DE
  SIRE            SIRE

            DEATH
```

Written By
TL SCHAEFER

Copyright © 2020 by Tyler Lee Schaefer

Original art and layout by Emily Poulin

All rights reserved. This book or any portion thereof may not be reproduced or used in any manner whatsoever without the express written permission of the author except for the use of brief quotations in a book review.

Printed in the United States of America

First Printing, 2020
ISBN 978-0-578-79126-5

www.tylerschaefer.com

For Mike (the Canadian Word-smith), Atch, and Bogie. The guides who've taught me what it means to seek.

"He's telling me to stand in the slow waters..."

The following work was created to reflect the way in which I find myself speaking with and pursuing God. This has come to be my pattern on this road of chasing. This road of seeking.

DESIRE

When God speaks, it starts in my chest and burns as a cigarette's cherry in the nighttime. Each inhale crackles and glows steady, as if it were suffocating for the next exhale. The next word. The next touch. It happens sometimes in conversation when words fly as swallows in a barn. Knocking loose the cobwebs and dust dumbly as they expose areas of the structure previously hidden. Previously known only to the builder. Sometimes it's a beauty that is struck so perfectly the reaction triggers a memory locked in the fabric of my DNA. A memory that travels thousands of generations and back to a garden of which I do not remember, yet I long for. Sometimes it's prayer, sometimes it's inaudible. Sometimes it's clean, other times it is in fact filthy. Sometimes it's a discipline and mundane. Sometimes it's spastic and indulgent.

When God speaks my entirety,
muscle and mind, roars with desire.

OUTER

The desire burns bright, but soon a draft of cooling remembrance sleepwalks through me. Noise from everywhere, opinions from everyone, dogma from the saints, heresy from the sinners, and even chirps from the birds begin to drown out that holy sound. I am reminded again of the world, of my home, and of the way it sounds. Of the ways it distracts. Electronic screens and algorithms. Pro this and pro that. Left and right. This church, that man. Movements and revolutions. I am a filter with the smoke traveling through me. Before I am flicked into the street, I am filled with the byproducts of consumption. Before long, God's voice is replaced by the confusion of every voice.

The outer influence pulls the desire and
I am left empty from the osmosis.

INNER

Once empty, the sounds dissipate as I close the door behind me. I am in an apartment complex with very thin walls. Each unit houses versions of myself, memories, or some kind of weird Frankenstein-esque combination of the two. There is a comfort here, with the door closed. A kind of comfort that kills. Through the sheet rock that separates my living space, I can hear my addictions arguing next door. On the other side of me, anxiety falls asleep with its TV on too loud, and the sound keeps me up all night. Here is where a chess game of trauma, shame, fear, and the like take turns within the lobes of my brain. There is no phone, there is no communication, and from deep inside I lose not only the desire but also the memory of God.

Inside myself, I find no hidden answer.
Just a deeper rabbit hole with taking me further from God.

DEATH

Like finding Colonel Kurtz on the inner thigh of the Congo, I must reach the dead end of my spiral. I must release the theology, bias, box, foolishness, or the like to see clearly again. Scales sliding off of the eyes, or the warm water from a spring type of molting. It feels as comfortable as a bullet through the chest might, and I hang on until I have tried every procedure to keep the old alive. I must allow there to be a death. Be it my expectations, or my pride. Be it my fear, or my shame. Be it anything and everything. I must go to God with emptied hands, with unburdened shoulders.

Death must occur as a cleansing. As a grace.
It must wipe clean the slate so gunked up by everything inside me and outside me.

LIFE

On the third day, he rose. Three of the women and I went to his tomb expecting to see his body and were frightened to find an angel instead. Why do I seek the living amongst the dead? I carry the spices to embalm a body not there, and in the bewilderment a glimpse is offered. The proof, or the answer, is rarely revealed straight on. Instead, a sort of growth from the newly torched-down forest is seen among the char. A relief is offered from the clipping of a rotting branch. A masterpiece is born from an unplanned stroke.

From the rubble of it all, there is a moment of clarity, there is a silhouette of the one my everything longs for.

The following work was created to reflect the way in which I find myself speaking with and pursuing God. The words are not perfect, nor their theology. Such things should not be perfect. At times, the words are crass and profane. Such things should be. In the pages that follow I speak in the voice God gave me, and with words I understand.

I dance naked before the Lord.

This has come to be my pattern. This is how I seek.

I dance naked before the Lord.

This has come to be my pattern. This is how I seek.

I WILL SEEK I

God, what cost is to be paid in seeking,
From the distance of mortality, peeking?
Was this your plan from the beginning?
Upside down victory, underdog winning.
Your son leaving,

For a world unbelieving.
Why do I forget yesterday for today?
Why do I find it so hard to trust what you say?
Your son leaving,
For a world unbelieving.
Red light, green light, red light,
Oh lord Jesus Christ — the darkest night,
Green light, red light, green light,
Am I saved still? Do we seem alright?

Your son leaving,
My heart unbelieving.

LIL MONSTERS

He cut the ties that bind
Machete mind
Made up and papers signed
Human tethers left behind.

Unfaithful yet proud
He can be himself again
Quiet ideas come loud
A fresh start — Brand. New. Him.

The heart wants what it does
It pushes and shoves
Drives drunk, pumps and loves
Snakes eating the doves.

Happiness is American. Christ's imposter
Our lord, pimp and sponsor.

Amen

I WILL SEEK

TL SCHAEFER

LUKE 1

Was it like saying goodbye at the airport?
Or before the cross country drive?
Boxes loaded in the car. Playlist primed.
Did your heart hurt?
Did it leap within you?

Were you sad? Were you proud?

I am a revolving door.
Finding myself not needing who you sent,
Finding myself not deserving of who you sent.

Can you forgive me for that?

Can you strike me silent?
Father to something I'm too foolish,
To accept.

Keep every word I have until,
I learn a name,
Not known to myself,
Nor father, nor kin.

Until I feel you leap within my stomach.
Making gestures,
Writing on a tablet, mute.
Lay awe on the neighborhood,
And make me into the man,
Unafraid of the wilderness,
Or the ministry outside of it.

Strong in spirit,
Seeking like Theophulis,
And family to the virgin's Son.

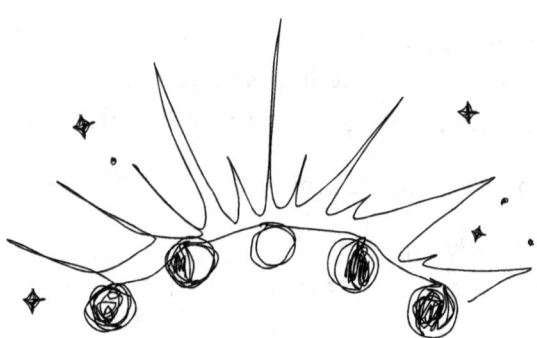

DAY ONE

The void stared into the void, inside out.
And then repeated, smiled and began to pout,
Uninhabitable, wild, scary, unsafe, or maybe not,
Someone shouting words, but not talking a lot,
Record players with fourteen needles, no records,
One giant empty, filled with finite hoards.
The void stared into itself, then again, then again,
The void talked to itself, then again, then again,
It was big and clumsy, all organized and clean,
And it all made sense if you know what I don't mean.

Chaos in the darkness, all wild and unknown,
Put into perfect order by one voice alone.

What does it even mean to separate the dark from the light?
And what sound is made when ripping the day from night?
Like an eternal orchestra all getting in tune, climbing the scale,
Did the light rise up slow, did the dark deepen as it fell,
How mighty was your grip on the contrast,
Was it your silhouette that the first shadow cast?

When the light bled, and the first morning began to sweat dew,
Did every molecule cry out, did every atom acknowledge you,
As you hovered above it all, three in one,
Did you catch its reflection in the eye of your son?

Oh my God, was it for us — the children of wrath,
That you split the dark in half?

UNTITLED 09/11/19

Erosion and time
have colored in the lines you drew.
Death and decay
— and in your absence, refined
into a mutated definition of elegance.

Even the destruction is beautiful.

My heart is heavy as it longs
for the beauty outside of time
beyond death

—for the garden.

How will the leaves sound
as the wind curves over them,
as we are all together again?

What does laughter sound like
when it cannot be taken away?

I've no words today
just a psalm spoken inside a chest,
wanting to lie across yours
and be rocked by the breathing
of a God who feels.

PSALM 51

Of twisted mind and heart,
In sunlight and dark,

I come, solely responsible,
My rebellion, rotten soul.
I come, fully aware,
My crimes, my face bare.

Oh Lord, give me water and hyssop,
Breathe into my bones, I give up.

Do not hide from me your voice,
I am finally broken — Oh God I rejoice.

I've confused bondage for beauty,
And your grace as cruelty.
Oh God, go gentle on me!

You don't want a sacrifice,
My rhetoric or religious device,
But my broken spirit shall suffice.

Open my lips, move my pen,
Wash me clean that I may speak to them,
Take pity on us, the suffering, similar men,
Build us, break us, defend,
That we may build a new altar then.

I WILL SEEK II

A world unbelieving, unworthy of such holy seeing,
Of a holy son, bruised up — coughing and bleeding,
Titans and planets, earthquakes, fire and pandemic,
Was the cost worth this? Each child a liar — condemn it,
Your bride's a whore,
It's not worth it anymore,
Do you see actually and clearly?
These people are monsters you hold dearly,
Your bride's a whore,
What are you coming back for?
Father, son, father,
Raped the mother, sold the daughter,
Father, son, father,
They are lambs, begging for slaughter.

Your bride's a whore,
Your people are rotten to their core.

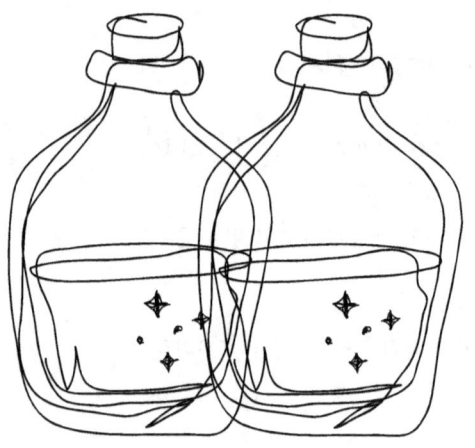

EVAN-JELLYFISH

Just behind your teeth
Back of throat
And underneath

You keep it all inside
Fearful
And tongue-tied

When you forfeit your voice
There is motive
There is a choice.

WOLF MAN

Wolfman, Wolfman sell to me,
Repackaged and processed,
Less sodium, sugar-free,

Sell me your tattoos and piety,
Pull the wool tight, hide your teeth,
Chop up and monetize Christianity,

Hold Jesus up for the shade,
Slot machine of Nazareth,
There's money to be made,

Wolfman rebrand me your cruci-fiction,
Make it ready for market,
Make true to me your fiction,

Make my payments easy and routine,
Make it exclusive and cold,
Make me beg to be on your team,

Rob us chumps of our change,
Hands tied up in prayer,
Faith lubricating the exchange,

I was raised with wolves like you,
The ones with no moon to howl to,
With claws that never grew in right,
Haunted by themselves at night,
I know the eyes you hide behind,
Hollow tunnels into a panicked mind,

The ones who felt safer amongst sheep,
Loathers of light, the midnight creep,
Dulling your fangs against the stone,
Lest you be seen, lest you be known,
I was bitten by wolves like you,
Gnawed on for years, nearly cut through,
Wolfman, Wolfman I can see you clearly,
I know your breath, I feel it near me,

My faith lies in the hope of a coming day,
When you are sold to no one willing to pay.

WASTED YOUTH GROUP

I hope that God is as mean,
As you made him out to be.
And I hope your heaven,
To be as far as you made me believe.

CHURCH

We hold this hope — pass it from hand to hand,
To every color, every woman — child and man.

Oh sweet bride, hope of the world do sing,

Here is the church, here is the steeple,
The world's hope is carried by people,
And they are precious in his sight,
Every shape and color from black to white.

Bride of Christ, hold my heavy mind,
Spit into the dust — we've grown blind.

How filthy the cross that saved me,
Perfection born low, made creaturely.
Beams of cedar absorbed the blood,
Of the broken heart, happily in love,
A tomb made liar, death made fool,
How sweet the grace, saved me, saved you.

How filthy the birth canal,
Fleshy and so very human as it doglegs,
Over the river Styx.

How many have died in the labor?
Crushed by the contracting walls.
Umbilical cord nooses and blue faces.

How many were washed clean?
Broken bags of water. Born again.
Naked and new.

Mother,

I pray there to be enough grace,
To forgive the bite marks,
I left on the breasts that fed,
My venomous and teething mouth.

Mother,

Can I hate the men you let stay the night?
The things you open your legs to?
The way they stand on your shoulders?

Whore,

Uncle Sam's pimping.
Show me the scars in Donnie's hands.
Let me feel the holes in his side.
Build a wall forever tall,
Discuss behind it what lives actually matter.
This is my vote, broken as bread.
This is my blood of new policy.
White church, Black church.
Red blush, blue eyeshadow.

Of whores and mothers,
I've come to know the Bride as both.
Two sides of the same coin.
Flipping.
Oh God your grace is a strange thing
And I own no aspect of it.

I WILL SEEK

Where was I when you painted your skies?
Or taught the sparrows to fly?
Or when you salted the ocean's guts?

Where was I those days you were dead?
Where was I when you walked through hell,
Saving those I'd have sent?

Where was I when you earned the grace,
I jockey to own.

Where was I when your spirit fell,
On your young bride as fury and flame?

I am a whore to my anger.
It leads me to hell by the ear.
Demanding each step.
I need a mother.
To hold me with diverse hands.
To speak to me in all languages.
To walk me home.

I pray your shoulders to be strong enough.
To carry the burdens that drown.
I pray your justice to be enough.
To sort all this out.
And I pray your grace enough.
To forgive us all the same.

Be me a whore.
Be me a mother.

FATHERS OF DEAD BABIES

Garden — God — falling doom
Cats in the cradle — silver spoon
A call — no answer — "Where are you?"
Man in the moon — little boy blue

Bunch of dead ass babies in the bin
Bunch of little boys, and no such men
Pandering, marching down main street
Prince virtue signaling, flavor of the week
Clipped balls, muzzled voice
Our mess — her choice

Only in a world of masculine silence
Can there be such a steady violence
These women are still washing our dishes
They're still cleaning up after our decisions

"Ask Eve, she gave me the fruit you see?
She ate it first, not me"

LUKE SEVEN

For whom is the alabaster tipped,
And who is sought by the Centurion?
For whom does the dead rise,
And who sees the widow?

Between the strands of brandy dyed hair,
Perfume bubbled and foamed,
Within a stone's throw.

Of those who thought your love fair,
A thing to be won or honed,
Quid pro quo.

But of her sins, you were aware,
Long list of what she owned,
Taken in tow.

Fragrance of faith, sweetly spiced the air,
Forgiving her debt once loaned,
Sweet chariot, swing low.

I WILL SEEK III

Though a whore, her hair smelled clean,
She sipped at a cigarette quickly — but not mean,
I cared not for her thoughts, nor her eyes,
I wanted her lips, I wanted her ribs — her thighs,
I raped the gospel,
Church turned brothel,
Us and them, saved and lost,
And I profiteered on your cost,
I raped the gospel,
Make me John the envious, Peter the hostile,
Praise me, raise me, praise me,
My soul grown fat — lazy,
Raise me, praise me, raise me,
I grabbed at your crown, confused and crazy,

I raped your gospel,
Your legacy and each apostle.

LUKE TEN

As the color of ink and brushstrokes,
her hair painted its way down the nape,
of her neck, cricked upward.

She watched Him with plain eyes,
and listened with mundane ears.

And He spoke plain,
to the mundane.

For the first time since her father,
had taken the long sleep,
since her black hair had been stroked,
by his sandpaper hands,
she felt her soul rest.

Complexities and long sleeps,
took a break from leaning,
against her tired mind.
Around the feet of a mystery named Jesus,
she was as a child come home.

Her sister, with hair drawn identical,
had placed her hands in the path,
blocking the way to his feet.
A path leading home. A way home.

There, in a home, between two sisters,
grace was shown to not be fair, nor bought.
It is not many things, but indeed one.
And no feet, nor hands,
can take it away.

GUILT, DOUBT, AND LINES IN THE SAND

GUILT
I fear the crucifix scalpel did not cut clean,
I fear that it left but a cell,
To infect, or split and grow into terminality,
It's been several years since that battlefield triage,
And I fear the infection dances through my blood,
Twisting its hips, twisting my guts,
Stamping its feet, stamping out my breath,

Because I feel as if I survived the war,
To be haunted by the dreams and defined by its wounds,
Apparent and invisible,
I can smell the gangrene, I feel the shrapnel in my spine,
The copper taste of blood on the back of my tongue,

I fear that the trenches I had to hide in,
The places I took shelter,
Are too deep for one to climb out of,
I fear those gaps are as a chasm to us,
I fear your arms too short to reach,
My arms too weak to wave,

I had to kill my brothers, I had to kill my friends,
We shared faces, we shared voices,
Melted lead through the lungs,
Cold bayonet through the windpipe,
Choking, pleading, and dying,
I had to kill my brothers,
Goddamn it, I killed my friends,

The civil war in my mind,
In my life,

The treaty has been signed, but there are pockets,
There are insurgents that meet in the dark places,
Propaganda posters of doubt plastered,
To the alleyways of my mind,
There are assassins, there are saboteurs,
There are enemies of the state,
They do not fight fair, they lie in wait,
Strap bombs to their chests, throw acid,
Shoot up schools, behead innocence,

They are many, and they are one.
They are guilt,
And they whisper into my ear at night,
And they suffocate my faith.

DOUBT

The parking lot and the church have one thousand miles between them sometimes. Sometimes, I'd rather burn the place down than belly-up to it. My feet turn into cinder blocks, and my heart is tungsten. Guilt gives birth to doubt and I am their midwife.

As I hold guilt's baby in my arms, I walk into the church. The baby is screaming and everyone is looking at me. Everyone knows the things that I have done; things they would never even think of. I try to comfort the baby but it's of no use. Perhaps I'd be better off outside. Just on the other side of the walls.

I feel more comfortable outside anyways. I always have. There is nobody out here looking at me or my baby. Perhaps the two of us are just better off out here. Perhaps everyone is better off with us out here.

So, I stay outside to raise somebody else's baby. Too afraid to speak. Too sure of my own evil to believe in grace.

This is my guilt and it's as big as boulders. This is my doubt and it swallows the ocean.

When they drug my broken body to you, you were kneeling in the sand. With your finger, you were writing something in the dust. They heaped my mass at your feet, and yelled my accusations. Through one swollen eye, I looked at their faces. All of them, the entire lot, was none other than myself.

For the next few minutes I was called an addict. I was branded a pervert. One version of myself had every foul thing I ever said tattooed into his skin. While another was wearing clothes that didn't fit him, screaming that I've ruined all my opportunities. Someone was holding a poster of every girl that I mistreated. Someone was reciting every lie I had ever told, and another was holding a receipt for my every cent spent on drugs.

You just kept kneeling, looking at whatever you were writing. Waving your finger through the dust.

All at once, they asked for your approval of my demise. They wanted your blessing to throw stones at me. Their hands, my hands, gripped the rocks. Their voices, my voice, called for blood.

You stood up, and said something about throwing the first stone. You asked only the innocent to throw. Eventually they, we, all left. There was no one around but you and myself.

You walked over to me,
I was the size of a mustard seed,
You looked down on my scars,
You reached down with your scars,
Asked if anyone had condemned me,
I shook my cloudy head, twisted my broken neck,
Good, you said, neither do I,
Go and sin no more,
And when the war rages in your mind,
In your life,
When you are holding the child of your guilt,
When that doubt is screaming in your arms,
Remember my words, remember my scars,
Remember when you were heaped at my feet,
And I drew lines in the sand.

LUKE 11

Some nights,
ghosts appear in the texture of the drywall,
fiends as animals created by bent shadow balloons.
And so, I see faith naked and true.
There are no flower petals, no hot pink,
no smooth coats, no fluff, nor ease.

I've got battleships in my brain,
glaciers around my lungs.
A lake of shame, an ocean of fear.
The things that didn't kill me,
have not made everything stronger.

Some nights,
I have but mustard seeds.

When I stand at the door and knock,
It's with a scrappy faith,
ribs showing through tissue paper skin.
Missing teeth, broken bones,
Open wounds.

When you open it,
it's with a love,
Audacious and shameless.

Hallowed be thy name.

SUCH OFFENSES AS THESE

Such offenses as these.

My resentments stand as cedar beams
Fallen descendants demand, thine bleeder screams

Forever won, "It is finished"
Song sung to forgiveness's cynics

My reasons, my walls, my protection
Meet me, O Sleeper, at thine cross section
As if answers could ease the infection
As if I could skip your crucifixion

Hell is no home for the guilty
We are all misunderstood and filthy
Dealt bad hands, loaded dice
From the men to the mice

I hold my hatred like a hammer, like nails
Recorded wrongs, canonized betrayals
My chains, my cell, my restraints
My tormentors became my saints

I would sell your son for explaining
Miss your death — complaining
Abandon your bride, naked and raining
Vomit out your spirit — blaming

O, the God who sees
Cut me down to my knees
Search me, know me underneath
Forgive such offenses as these,
My bitterness, my boiling disease
It stands as cedar beams
Begging for the wrath it needs
Covered in a love that bleeds
Earned by the King of Kings.

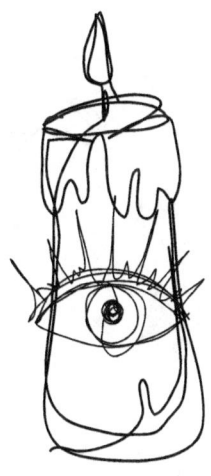

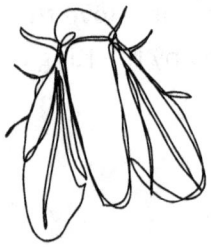

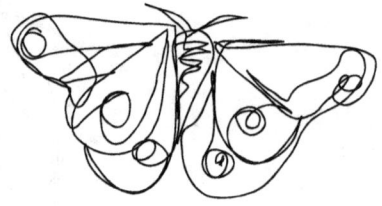

FOSTER KIDS

In confusion and shame, I have worked out my salvation.
As I cross the minefield of repentance with stone feet.
The earth sucking as I lift the weight of myself.
I used to stand up but now I crawl on my belly,
Towards the razor wire of my lusts, unable to dig,
Deep enough to escape from underneath their thumb.

Born into this place by the dust you spun.
By the people you made. By the people they made.
All of us foundlings looking for a way back home.
Latch-keyed by a sickness we all share.

And as such you have adopted me.
Pulling me from the mud, wiping my face.
Cleaning the filth and shouldering the weight.
And instead of praising you for it,
We argue what your motivation was for the adoption,
Who chose who, and eligibility for selection.
While the other orphans drown unaware of their hope.
Laying tulips on their grave, as to make it easier to understand.
As if there is sense to be made of such things.

I don't feel at home in my new house.
I don't like my new brothers and sisters.
There is a difference between us.
And I can't let my guard down.

I was adopted before this.
By a family of wolves dressed up like sheep.

Where every wall of the house was lined,
With bunk beds and rhetoric.
Where each child was espoused for a check.
The souls became numbers and together,
The body ate itself. It still does. They still do.
I was made into the feces that it passed,
After I crawled up its spine,
Begging for help. Begging for a father.

I was returned to the agency.
It wasn't a good fit, I guess.
In silence they left me on the doorstep.

What if this happens at my new home?
What happens when the wolves come back?
And if I am supposed to find my hope in you,
Why did you leave man to carry it?
What part of us was made in your image?

Do I have to call you dad?
Do I have to play with the other kids?

I barricade myself in the room you gave me.
Locking it from both sides. For fear.
For fear of what the other kids might be.
For fear of what I might do to myself with the freedom.
Is this the home you wanted?
A house full of fear and pretend?
When we come to the table for dinner,
Who do we come as?
Through the walls of my fortified room I scream.

Give me back to the pigpen of the damned.
Let me find the birth canal to crawl back through.
Give me back into the womb in which we are made.

Why must you stay just out of sight?
Like a deadbeat dad who shows up,
When it works out for him.

There are times I accuse you,
Of adopting me too late.
That the things I did to survive,
Killed anything good left inside me.
And that one day,
I'll be left on that doorstep again.

As alone as I was,
When I came into this world.

What took you so damned long?

It is in fear and trembling that I come to my doubts.
In their confession I feel split open. I hold them in my hands.
I hold them as my hidden things, new to the light.
Can I hate the distance between us freely?

Don't leave me to my doom, I beg you!
Don't see me as I see myself.
I am a dog with yesterday's vomit,
Warming up in the microwave.
I have several portions for the week.

I WILL SEEK

And I will return to what kills me,
Again, and again, and again.
The golden calves and the praise of men.
The thirty pieces of silver for a kiss,
Bathsheba on the roof, naked and beautiful.

Can I hate the evil inside of me?

When a child is adopted,
There is a choice made, an action done.
It pulls the orphan into something new.
Making them into a member of a family.

I think our family is something I can start to understand.

But your grace is harder to explain, harder to say.
But I think it's a place to exist and stay,
Like a harbor's arms or the mouth of a bay,
To find refuge in the sand and to lie or lay.
It takes the ones thrown out, without a home,
The orphan, broken, blemished, and alone,
Who are rotten to the core, to the bone,
With eyes as glass and hearts as stone,
The people the world calls a monster,
Seeing them as one more perennial to foster.

ZOBOOMAFOO

Yellow morning light as scrambled eggs
Like our hair
A Saturday morning's yawn steeping
PBS Kids
Back when TVs were inside cabinets
Back when nothing was on demand
Nor downloaded.

Innocence fell like manna
Fell from the knockdown textured walls
It piled up as pillows for me and my sisters
To rest upon.

And I am not sure what I miss most:

Phones tied to walls
TV's inside cabinets
Egg-soaked rest
The single roof over us
Or that lemur puppet we'd watch.

I WILL SEEK IV

The sheets smelled sweet, perfume stuck around,
As my breath dropped, chest sunk down,
In came the hooded demon, sickle in hand,
Black teeth clicked as the grave told of his final demand,
Death ate me right up,
And I swam in his acidic gut,
Blackness, nothingness in the void,
Nothing left to learn or be enjoyed,
Death ate me right up,
And you poured out your righteous cup,
Falling, falling eternal,
My family calling from the inferno,
Falling, falling — eternal
O hell is deep, O hell is eternal

Death swallow me up,
Despite my works, despite my luck.

FURY

I was told the Devil threw firey darts
That he hid in darkness,
Had horns and a tail.

My God, I can't see Satan for the trees,
Snipers in the timber, bolt action,
hot lead rips flesh, cooks the fat.

Machine gun fire from the craters,
left by the bombs we dropped,
They're dug deep in the earth
Mud men, spun dust spitting-
— even foxes have their holes.

Tracers every three rounds, light up the dying sunset
momentary daylight, flashes of escape.
And I want just one to catch my skull,
Bounce back and forth,
Push the froth of my brains out the exit.

My expectations are lying.
Dying.

Holding purple ropes of intestines,
Missing portions of their faces,
Spattered in blood, crimson criers.

There are no reinforcements here.
Just thoughts
Just bayonets
Just bullets.
I was told the devil was red,
I was told not to fear him,
For you would protect me.

I WILL SEEK

In this abandoned place,
this war zone — I am alone.
Clinging to a rifle, stock of cedar.
magazine holding three bullets as one.
my friends are dead
my leaders are cowards
my mind is occupied
my body is failing
my God is seconds long — moments big.

Boots stamping the ground,
They are running
I am hiding.

Is this what victory is?
Narrow escape
Haunted survival?

I was told the devil was crafty,
but I don't see him hiding,
He's not behind the clouds,
He's not a prayer away.

He straddles my mind,
advances into my soft parts,
and sounds just like me.

Death, if i give you my hand,
Do you promise to break the circle?
Could it be quick?
Could I get some sleep?
Could you show me rest?

God, you've laid me down in doomed pastures,
Told me not to worry,
As I'm eaten alive, screaming and pleading
by this fallen fury.

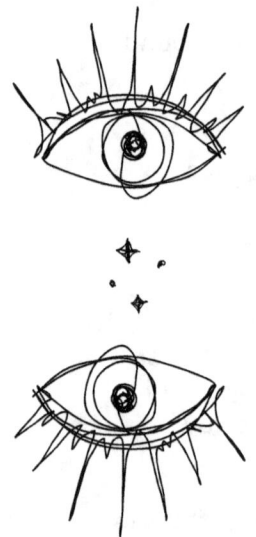

DON'S WAKE

Jesus movement music as funeral dirges,
The hippies have gotten old, and so have I.
How I knew your songs well in my youth.
I thought of that youth, and the man we mourned.

You people never liked to dress up,
Even now, you dress for leisure not lament,
I think I have always liked that,
You people made that aspect of God approachable. At least.

Death is a loud-mouthed kid, clumsy and heavy,
It's voice is abrasive, and it stings like hell,
We talk about it now, different churches,
Conflicting theologies,
Similar tears in the same room,
Holy Spirit underneath a T-bar ceiling,
Moving.

A Vietnam vet spoke like a man,
About a man,
Two daughters, about their father,
A beautiful young girl, about her role model,
An even younger girl,
Who felt the sting of Death's abrasive voice,
For the first time,

Death lasts a lifetime, like a stain.

We are all the same,
Reckless and stupid as hell,

Our ideals like buoys in an ocean of confusion,
I pray that one day the youth forgive me,
The way I must with these old hippies,
May I drown in forgiveness,

We all need it.

The dead man, and your only son,
Both left behind legacies of hope,
A hope that steps over bias,
And chokes out death.

Though we often have different perspectives,
We still cling to it in the same way,

Because you are God, and we are not.
Because you died so we might not.

DINO LINT

Dear death,
The bed's gone.
The one we'd watch him on.
From either side,
From so far away,

I watched as you made him into a child again.
As his son bathed him
As he was fed like a baby
By his baby.

What a cruel thing it is,
For eternal things to end.

And now the bed is gone
— just like him.
You traded us silence,
Force fed us the absence.

I've got mustard seeds
That once you're done
Bruising our heels,
A nail-scarred foot
Will crush your fucking head.

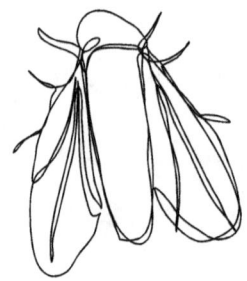

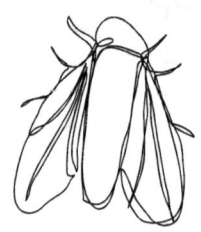

FIFTH OF JULY

Everything outside smelled like a gun.
Snapping, spitting, exploding,
There were no stars in the sky.
No shine through the smoke.

Sometimes what truly kills us,
Does so in the space between
Now and stronger.

I slept in a car then,
When a couch could not be found.
Between Denver's teeth
I was homeless in many ways,
And the thought was growing as a weed,
In my mind's dirt.

It flowered that morning,
Petals opened up like a firework,
Shooting sparks, illuminating everything.
In the sound of its bloom,
I found peace.

Broken, with no intention of fixing,
The shatter I saw as worthless,
Suicide came to me as a nurse.
Veiled and sweet, she spoke down to me.
She asked to lead me away,
Somehow, someway, I decided to stay.

One more sunrise.
One more day.

Life is a gun,
Snapping, spitting, and exploding.
It's the fifth of July,
A hangover of yesterday's elations.
It's waves breaking over the broken.
Some nights the stars are hidden by smoke,
Some nights they bleed into your home.

Hope, however, is not a gun.
It snaps not, nor spits.
Hope does not explode.
It stands steady amongst the tide.
Burns as a star one can follow home,
A star one can see through
The smoke.

Hope speaks upwards, unveiled.
The way a father might,
To a child afraid of something,
They can't see past.

Hope is one more sunrise,
One more day.
It's water breaking at midnight,
It's handwritten vows,
Stories of how they met,
Years sober, days clean,
Friendly dogs on a walk,

I WILL SEEK

Hope is falling off the wagon,
The first day, for the fifth time,
Hope is having the hard talk,
Getting your heart broken,
Starting over,
Moving out with nothing,

Hope is staying.
Despite the snapping, spitting, explosions.

DEATH

Crimson lines followed the grain,
Down the cedar beam as they crawled
At the base they collided and pooled.

Blood mixed with the dust,
As the dust
You spun watched.

I've no way to make sense of it,

The collision of love and pain,
Cross point between your shoulders,
Behind you — out of your sight—
Looking onward.

Behind you, like where you place my sins,
Like where you leave my mistakes,
Like something I cannot make sense of,

You bear grace in a way
None of my other gods can,
My chains have yet to bleed,
On my behalf —
For my sake.

You find my heart heavy
As iron in the ocean.
Lost in the caterwaul
Of disingenuous saviors, GMO truths
And the great pimps of the flock.

Who bleed for no one
Who bear nothing.

I've made a golden palace, cruel and jagged,
From the pieces of trauma,
Where I can hide and float,
My god of justification
My god of exclusivity
— that doesn't bleed
Unless I bleed first.

Boil me down to the bone,
Tear the meat with claws
And grind me back into dust

Pool crimson over my entirety
Lay upon me grace
In a way I'll never understand
Nor deserve.

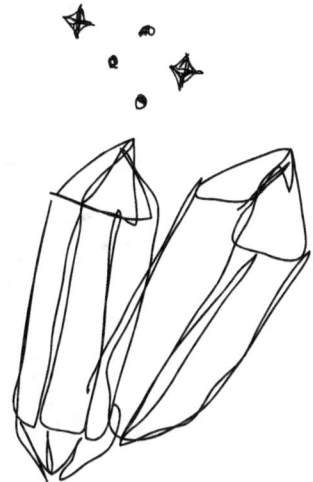

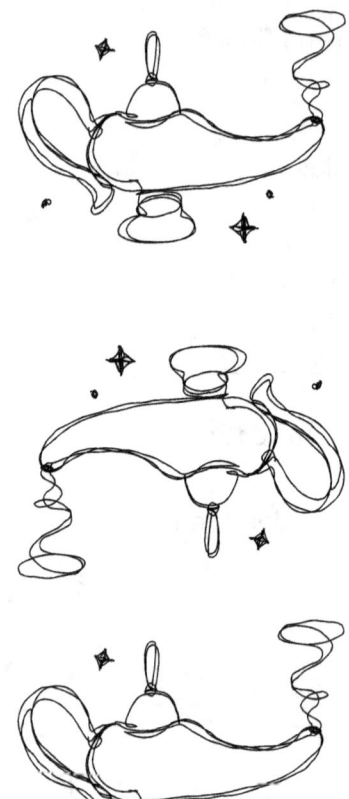

GOOD FRI-YAY

Slithering continuous, you steady breather
Asbestos breath, melanoma coat

The stillborn's mother, the geriatric's promise
Car accident opportunist,
Warlord's porno.

You drag your belly toward us all
Scaly and vile, man's cursed snake
Man's reward — namesake
Test results rhythm, tragic dancer,
The changing subject, climax prancer

Relieving end of suffering,
Starting point for secondhand pain,
We feed you, we feed you
We feed you, we feed you

Death, what does your hunger feel like?
That gnawing intestinal bite.

You graze like a bull
In this field called time
Where each blade of grass
Is a story, is a creation
Where each blade gets smashed,
Rolled up against your golden molars,
Smoothed out with your concluding tongue
And somewhere between stomachs
You find we all taste the same to you

That same barnyard sod feel

King and orphan, priest and felon
Old and young, black and white
Those ready for you
Those dragging their feet
Apathetic eyes peer down a pitch black snout
Above polished teeth clipping away
At the mortal lawn under your hooves

All the while a Jewish matador
was sharpening a cedar saber

But death fears no man —
Even the perfect one

From its foul mouth and forked tongue
From its sulfur lungs, it asked —

"Why do you blame me,
For my existence,
Am I not the craft of your children?
Is not the paste on their hands red?"

It was then- they placed the first nail in his wrist
Right next to the scar he had received
As a young man, learning to plane a beam
Learning to work with wood, learning a trade
Being taught.
The nail stuck into his flesh like a saber
Into the beast.

I WILL SEEK

His mother, watching, remembered
A time before he was a carpenter
Before he was a man.
She remembered the way his rib cage
Would fit in her arms —

— it didn't today as it hung up in the air
Gulping for breath, panicking for breath.
Bruising and cramping as his mortal body failed
His spine sagging against the timber

Muscles as stones, organs as sand.

He took the bread and broke it
This is my body

Type B dripped down the cross
Spinning in the knots as hard as alabaster
The sky spun itself insane — firefly flux
Soldiers and citizens, universal donors
Jew and gentile

Systemic arterial flow, nailed to wooden filth
The carotids worked overtime
Losing pressure, hemorrhaging and leaking,
Crimson steams rolled against the bark,
Ducking into the grooves left by the saw
Racing down toward the dirt at the base.
Dropping toward the earth
Falling against his creation
Running to his work

Then he took the cup and gave thanks —
This is my blood.

Death stamped its hooves through the dust
Tattooed belly dragging through the crowd
It curled its tongue around the man from Nazareth
Unhinged its jaw and got ready
As the ground shook, it swallowed the man
-and into death's throat he fell.
The heart stopped, and death wandered on.

Onto its next meal, onto its duty

From inside its bowels there was a commotion
A pain,
Death hoped it to be indigestion
It tried to ignore the stinging in its guts
But on that day, even death knew
It had eaten something
the motherfucker couldn't stomach.

GOOD FRIDAY REDUX

O Death, where is thy sting?
Where are your molars — your biting?
Of the bodies you stack and hoard,
Bless the One that ruined your record.

O Death tell me, how did it feel to die?
Did you beg and scream. Did you cry?
Of the bodies you stack and hoard,
Humiliated by the One — the Risen Lord.

Oh, you coward speak up — I can't hear,
Bodied in the street, no help nor tear,
The Lion of Judah, Almighty God, heavy on your head,
The pierced hands that meticulously made your bed,
Now sleep in it!
Get deep in it!
Silent and bitch-made, come crawling,
Listen, boy, your daddy is calling,
Crawl on all four to Him, kiss His feet,
Roll over, sit down, and learn defeat,
He ripped from you everything, all glory all praise,
And you, you tired little rat you, got three days.

O Death, I ask again, where is thy sting?
How glorious does He look — our King?
Of the bodies you stack and hoard,
Ransomed by Jesus Christ and restored.

O Death, on this day you broke off your own confused face,
Trying to swallow perfection, choked on amazing grace,
Shattered into oblivion under His unending throne,
Unable to break Him, not even a single bone.

It is finished.

I WILL SEEK V

Death vomited and I was drowning in the bile,
And redemption met me with a smile,
When I deserved everything but what was given,
Jesus Christ bathed me, called me forgiven,
What is this grace?
This moment suspended in space,
I was meant for flame,
Called out of hell by name,
What is this grace?
This love that took my place,
I don't deserve, I don't deserve any of it,
Abundance it flows, plenty of it,
I don't deserve, I don't deserve any of it,
Not known for the evil I've done — or yet to commit.

What is this grace?
Oh God, how beautiful your face.

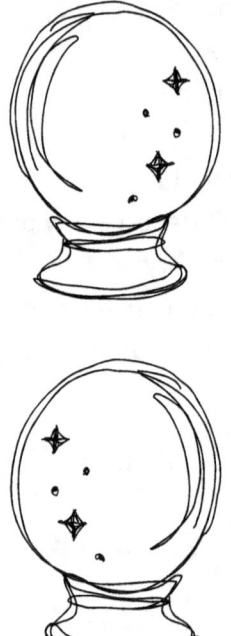

AN EASTER PSALM

Looking for the living amongst the dead,
My story, the prodigal that fled,
Doomed to a demise of my own making,
A life lost and defined by my forsaking,
But amazing is your grace, and sweet the sound,
That took in a wretch like me, made me found.

Looking to make living out of the dead,
Your story, a body broken up like bread,
Smashed up face, thorns stuck in your head,
Lighting bolts of pain, wounds that bled,
You became just like me, my people,
And subjected yourself to our ways, our evil,
That amazing grace, and that sound so sweet,
Two nails for the hands, one for the feet.

Look at the living that rose from the dead,
That ripped the veil in half, spun sin on its head,
Defeated the grave, choking death on its tongue,
Darkness was met with light and undone,
How sweet that deafening sound, that amazing grace,
Death's champion and life's embrace,
That promises to raise us again, bathed in glory,
This is our hope, our story.

PSALM 54

¹*Save me, O God, by thy name, and judge me by thy strength.*
    My voice is quiet, my mind is loud,
    God, I'm not too shy nor too proud,
    Sticks and stones, have broken my every last bone,
    Can you come over? I don't want to be alone,

²*Hear my prayer, O God; give ear to the words of my mouth.*
    Through the TV static, under the powerlines,
    Across the saline deep, between the needle pines,
    Though my words are clunky and unclean,
    Please hear my heart, understand what I mean,

³*For strangers are risen up against me, and oppressors seek after my soul: they have not set God before them. Selah.*
    God they call you a hoax, lie, and a fraud,
    They cut my belly open, and inside me they maraud,
    My name is ruined by theirs, stabbed by lies,
    They fear no Lord, have no ties,

⁴*Behold, God is mine helper: the Lord is with them that uphold my soul.*
    Yet underneath your wing, within your fold,
    Beneath your shelter, gripped by your hold,
    You make healthy my mind,
    You pluck out the hooks, cut away all that may bind,

⁵*He shall reward evil unto mine enemies: cut them off in thy truth.*
    I take solace in the idea, I find peace in the fact,
    That when you come, you will leave none intact,
    You will lay waste to the hoard outside my gate,
    You will destroy the ones who lie, steal, and hate,

⁶*I will freely sacrifice unto thee: I will praise thy name, O Lord; for it is good.*
    With both hands twisted outward, palms out,
    I offer to you alone, with no hesitation — no doubt,
    And in continuation of what I do as habit and duty,
    I will praise your name alone, your beauty

⁷*For he hath delivered me out of all trouble: and mine eye hath seen his desire upon mine enemies.*
    On your back I traveled across the river Styx,
    As my enemies try by way of boats, mortar or bricks,
    Behind us they sunk into the water like stones,
    And as they reached the bottom, you walked on their bones.

THINGS I FORGOT

The things I forgot,
Are things I want,

Sunrises here are orange and blue,
Some sunsets are too,

The things I've said,
The wounds that have bled,

I am sorry God, I am sorry now,
Come tomorrow, though, I'll forget how,

I want you, need you and desire,
Through the snow, sleet, ash, and fire,

My lungs want to hold you,
My fingers want to fold for you,

My chest burns like a white coal,
It burns through my ribs, into my soul,

God, I have done and asked a lot,
Remind me of the things I forgot.

I WILL SEEK

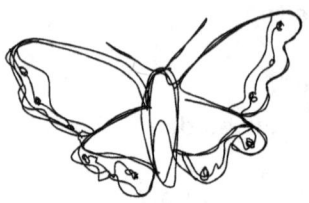

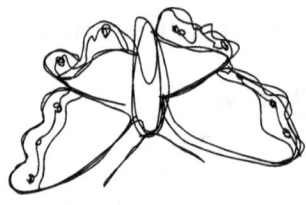

SWEET AT LAST

My faith — a child's grasp
I never knew to ask
I never knew how vast
My God — my sweet at last

I WILL SEEK

WRESTLING

On the fourth day
Dopesick and destroyed
I reached up with skinny arms
And wrapped my hands like a prayer
Behind your neck
Pulling my body against yours

I sunk my chin into your back
Our ribs rubbed and legs tied
We rolled like a knot
And I prayed like a machine gun

The poppy's roots were deep
And the heroin was no hero

My body was an ember

I prayed unholy and sweaty
We wrestled and spun

And there was profanity
Sickness and withdrawal
We spoke and I begged

Flesh to flesh
I struck at you
And you wore the hits

You've never been weak
And you've never held me any way
Other than a father might.

LUKE 24

You didn't leave
But you didn't stay

You didn't answer my questions
But you didn't need to

And in this moment, they float into the sky,
Between the clouds,
The ones you spoke into being
The ones that don't leave
But don't stay either

I asked for forgiveness
And you gave me yourself
I am a witness to these things

I asked for reasons
And you gave me grace
I am a witness to these things

I asked for destruction
And you became a father
I am witness to these things

Mystery shrouds the silhouette
Of a face my bones long for
My marrow boiling
Wonder blooms about your tongue
As it stirs my guts into flame
Does not my chest burn when you speak?

I WILL SEEK

Does not my soul beg?
Does not my being seek?

You didn't leave
And I didn't either
You didn't answer my questions
— you eclipsed them
And in this moment
I float in the place behind my eyelids
The ones you spoke into being
My most intimate hiding place
That we don't have to leave ever

Dancing naked before you
In your temple.

Amen

I WILL SEEK

I WILL SEEK REDUX

There is no understanding the cost,
Of your son going out to us — the lost,
Or my mother who may also be a whore,
Who I must love, who I must care for,
Forgive me for the box I've put you inside,
My foolishness the walls, my audacity its size,
Death comes for me, I accept my price,
And through you, I shall not be eaten twice.
I've given up on understanding your grace,
But never will I tire, of seeking your face.

www.ingramcontent.com/pod-product-compliance
Lightning Source LLC
Chambersburg PA
CBHW051408290426
44108CB00015B/2209